1ˢᵗ Edition 2022

ISBNs
Paperback: 979-8-9855709-3-9

EBook:
     Kindle 979-8-9855709-2-2
     EPub 979-8-9855709-1-5

Printed in the United States of America

When you begin your natural building journey your focus is on the building. Somewhere along the way your heart is filled with the wonderful realization that it is not about the building itself, but the sense of community the natural building has brought to you.

Cat Taylor

Dedication

This book is dedicated to my Husband, a Vietnam Veteran, Father and Grandpa.
The man that didn't even flinch when I said I wanted to build a house out of mud.

I love you, Jackie!

Jack Taylor
August 1947 - August 2021

Contents

Foreword

By Margaret Taylor

You never know where life is going to take you. I certainly never imagined myself living the life I'm now experiencing. The last seven years have been quite an inward journey, but there's also been a lot of outward exploration, too.

The inward exploration started when my husband was diagnosed with terminal brain cancer in 2012 and soon after losing him, corporate America and I parted ways. Was this it? What is life all about? Why are we here? My questions led me to yoga. I didn't anticipate it becoming such a focal point in my life, but it changed my world and my mind. After doing a couple of amazing yoga certifications in the US I took myself to the heart of it all. By 2017 I was at an Ashram in India ready to master hatha yoga at the Isha Yoga Center. After an intense 21 weeks I had earned my yoga teacher training certification which was very impactful and transformational. It left me with a greater sense of life internally, but my outside world didn't reflect this. Things needed to change, but I didn't know what that change was meant to be. I was still searching for more. This led to my outward exploration.

In 2021 I accompanied a friend traveling around the US looking for somewhere to call home. That was when I attended a workshop at Cob Hill and I never left. Cat has everything in Cob Hill I was seeking, but that I believed would not be possible to find. A special place to build a yoga retreat center where people can experience Classical Hatha Yoga and escape from the noise of life, a place more centered on giving than receiving, where people leave feeling empowered and happy.

I love the whole ethos of NaturalBuildingOrg, Cat has a very generous nature and wants to give back. They say the last phase of our lives should be about service to others. Life has been good to me and I'm ready for the rest of my life to be about service to others. I see a bright future for Cob Hill and all it has to offer and am super excited to have found this place.

The fact that Cat and I both have the same last name through marriage, are both widows of a similar age, are both passionate about service to others is so serendipitous. I can't wait to see where this leads us!

While this book has been a collaborative effort, the words and experiences are all Cat's, and I hope to be a knowledgeable natural builder myself in a few years. I've certainly come to the right place for this to happen! An aspiring yogi working with the earth everyday just feels so right!

Preface

At the end of 2012, my husband and I bought a fixer upper home on two acres. The home had been foreclosed and was in dire need of a lot of tender loving care. The backyard had an inground swimming pool, that after four years of sitting stagnant held four feet of sludge, minnows, snakes and frogs.

My daughter and I began the extremely dirty job of emptying and cleaning it out. My intentions were to change the pool design from chlorine to a natural chemical free pool system. The pool would include two large waterfalls. I was extremely excited to be building these out of sculpted cement. I have been an artist my entire life and sculpting is my favorite form of expression.

After completing my natural swimming pool, I was hired to do this for other people. In 2015 I was online searching for something related to natural pools and a screen full of cob homes popped up. This was how I discovered natural buildings. I was immediately obsessed with learning everything I could about it. The idea of having the freedom to sculpt my own home was like a dream come true!

Unfortunately, within months of discovering natural building I was diagnosed with breast cancer. Two years later, still weak from recovering from surgeries I loaded up and drove to Oregon to attend a building with cob workshop.

Even though during the time I had been down with cancer, I read every book and watched every video I could get my hands on. I felt I needed to affirm what I had learned in person, with a hands-on workshop. This was a wise decision, because even after having 25 years of experience with remodeling homes I needed the workshop to give me the confidence to build my own home.

After closing on our newly acquired 50 acres here in the Piney Woods of Northeast Texas I kicked off my build with a 10-day workshop. Also present was the Discovery Channel filming the build for their tv series "Building off grid".

A fun pic of us with the Discovery Channel film crew

Thankfully, I had help from some of the talented natural builders I met while attending the workshop in Oregon. Among them was the powerhouse couple of Adriana and Miguelito. They led the teaching of the 10 day workshop freeing me up to do more work on the build.

I also traveled and participated in several builds and demonstrations while doing my own build. These experiences have shown me that natural building is an ever growing, ever changing process.

There were still so many things I had questions about as I built my home. Some things I learned the hard way. I also learned that some things were not as technical or as difficult as they were originally presented to me. I do have a difficult time converting print into a mental picture when it comes to written instructions.

I wanted to create a book containing some of the building steps you may not retain or remember after taking a workshop. I have even included an area for taking notes at the end of each chapter for your own builds. There are many pictures to help visualize the concepts better. I have kept it simple and easy to understand. This book is by no means meant to be an "all you need" for building. This is more of a cheat sheet guide for retaining the information you learn in a workshop. I want to share with you what I have learned about natural building, and all the mistakes I made to help you to avoid these mistakes.

Acknowledgements

Since May 2018 I have had many wonderful people come into my life. It's a community where we all learn, support, and help each other. I could never have accomplished any of this without the infinite love and support of my husband, Jack Taylor.

A special thanks to Margaret. Without her awesome editing, design and computer skills I could never have completed this book. She came into my life at the right time and kept me sane after losing my beloved Jackie.

Thanks to Kaya for her dedicated support and for being the yin to my yang. A huge thanks to Ian for his hard work, loyalty and dedication.

Also, a special thank you to Willow and Michael for their editing, photography skills and for being so willing to help with every task put in front of them.

NaturalBuildingOrg has a wonderful Board of Directors who encourage me to continue moving forward and I'm incredibly grateful for them - Melissa, Judy, Sandi, Margaret.

A special shout out to Mike and Nalini for inspiring me to dream even bigger than I already do, and of course all the alumni students that are out there building their dreams after attending my workshops. You are the reason I do this!

There are so many more I am grateful for, there are not enough pages.

I want to thank everyone who has touched my home and my heart.

Introduction

Welcome to the world of natural building!

I am assuming since you are reading this book you have an interest in learning more about natural building. This book is a general overview of issues you may experience during your build. Whether it be questions or mistakes, they were learned the hard way by me, Cat Taylor.

Before we get in depth with any details, let's go over what the phrase natural building means - at least to me anyway.

There is the obvious "using only natural materials;" that is, no toxic materials, paints or cement. Does that mean you can't use any of these in your build? No, but it is preferred. There are people that can carry out the "all natural" easily, but not everyone has the capabilities in their area. You can incorporate some (un)natural into your build but be aware that natural and unnatural are incompatible, there will always be a consequence, or reaction. For example, you may get away with using concrete for a stem wall, but if you plaster a cob wall with concrete, the plaster will fall off as it is repelled away by the cob which needs to breathe. The cement stops the cob from breathing resulting in a separation.

One of my favorite meanings of natural building is the ability to build with your hands, naturally. There are no blueprints or strict lines or connections. You can add or change designs and walls as you build. You have the freedom to design your own home in a way that fits your own likes and needs.

There is so much more to natural building than you can ever imagine! The process brings back the sense of community that we as a civilization have lost, but still unknowingly crave. It creates team building skills and will bring out the artistic creativity in people that never knew they had it.

One of the most exciting days of my build was the day I finished the roof!
If I had to do it all over the roof would have been first.

One of my favorite aspects of building my own cob home is knowing firsthand where every wire, pipe or connection is because I put it there myself. I don't need to call "the guy" to fix anything or find my leaks. I know because I put it in myself and understand how it works. This is so empowering!

When you buy a home, utilities are often a mystery, you do not know where the plumbing, electrical, septic or anything is run in the walls or floors. You are at the mercy of paying someone to come out or try to guess. You have nothing invested in the house but money. There is no personal value or attachment, the house is a structure you live within.

When I am inside my bale/cob home, I feel a heartfelt personal attachment to every part of the home, it is itself an extension of myself, built with caring, loving and determined hands. Everyone that put time in my home, also put love and dedication into it and it shows. There is no greater feeling, especially for an artist, to live within their greatest sculpture.

As you travel down the path of natural building, you will have many questions. This will never change. There is really no such thing as an expert because nature is not consistent, nor is the earth below our feet. Building a natural home will be different for everyone depending on location, terrain, weather and more. The object is to learn the basic principles and goals and then adapt them to fit your environment. There is no set recipe or rules, only "roughly right", and that works for natural building. Let me explain, when I attended a natural building workshop in Oregon, the focus was on building to create solar gain and bring in the heat from the sun to warm the home. This is a wonderful concept for a region that is primarily cold throughout the year with a short mild summer. I had to take the information I learned and adjust it to my region's weather, which is quite the opposite. Here in Texas, we have predominantly hot weather with short mild winters. I had to design my home to keep the heat out in the hot months. It was not hard to figure out. Once you have taken a good workshop and done a bit of research, it is only common sense. There are no limits, or step by step instructions for building, you are free to design, create and build however you want. There are however common-sense guidelines to keep your build safe, sturdy and lasting for hundreds of years to come!

Every day I learn something new about building naturally. It is a never-ending learning process and an on-going challenge. This is my absolute favorite thing about it!

Natural Building - never boring, always changing, never the same.

If you have never stepped into a cob home, I highly recommend you do. There is no comparison to the fresh, clean, earthy and nontoxic air you breathe! It is more of a feeling of living with the home versus living inside it. You have built your home with your own hands, sweat, sometimes blood and tears. The home is a part of you, and you are one with your home, now that is something to come home to! This may sound so spiritual and naive, but it's an experience of connection. You can really feel this connection when you step into a cob home.

Relaxing and enjoying the benefits of cob after an exhausting day of building can be enjoyable for the whole family.
Notice the spiderweb cracks in the cob. Since the camera crews needed a smooth finish for television I left the cob mix at a high clay content, giving surface cracks for the plaster to grab hold of.

Don't stress yourself out with a deadline, take your time and enjoy the process. It can be slow and grueling on a sweltering day. But the result is so worth the effort. You can set goals, but don't depend on them. Make sure you know what you are doing before you start. Don't set yourself up for failure.

I can tell you from experience that even though I spent two years watching videos and reading every book I could get my hands on, it wasn't enough. Not until I solidified what I had read with a hands-on workshop was I ready to do my build.

Although I understood the basics when I started my first build, I still make mistakes and continue to learn as I keep building. The wonderful thing about natural building is that it is so forgiving, so if you make a mistake, it is fixable and doesn't cause a failed build. The only exception to that would be if it were built on an extremely incorrect foundation. After all, the foundation is what your entire build rests on for stability and support.

This is why I have designed the structure of our ten day workshops the way I have. Most workshops will have the foundation done when you arrive. Even though how it was built is explained to you, it doesn't give you hands-on knowledge and experience. This may leave unanswered questions. I was a bit unsure of my foundation and did have to reach out with questions and concerns, but I nailed it in the end!

After experiencing the trials and tribulations of doing a build I have tried to share all my mistakes and learning moments. Doing this, maybe I can help someone else avoid these pitfalls and thus have a smoother, more enjoyable building experience.

There are so many natural building projects and skills that are not covered in these pages. There are subjects and skills that deserve their own book, including natural plasters, cob ovens and rocket mass heaters. There are already some great reads available on all these subjects, and I encourage you to check them out. I can tell you firsthand that the master artisan of natural plasters is Athena Steen. As you continue to absorb the teachings of all the natural builders out there, remember that there are a lot of distinctive styles of doing things. There is no exact right or definite wrong, just roughly right. Roughly right is all you need for success in a natural build.

Again, this book is not a step-by-step instruction manual for building your house. This is a guide and overview of the natural building process. There are optional pages for notes at the end of every chapter.

These 'notes' pages allow you to add any pertinent information about each subject, either learned from one of our workshops, an experience, or while attending a mother earth fair natural building seminar.

I hope you enjoy this book, and I hope to meet you as you start down the path of natural building.

Building a natural path to healing.

Myths and Facts

Myth: The most common myth in cob and straw bale building is - "I can't build with cob or straw here, it is too wet, humid, hot, cold or it snows too much here!"

Fact: As with all builds, you must build according to your local climate. The first and foremost rule with using cob and natural clay plasters is a '**good hat and boots**'.

Your roof (the hat) should have a long enough overhang to protect your walls from the constant beating of rain. The foundation (the boots) protects the inside from water entering your home and supporting the massive weight of your cob structure. The correct foundation and stem wall will lift your walls up and away from the dangers of any water damage.

Cob—a mixture of clay, sand, straw and water--is a strong and breathable material that can withstand years of getting damp. The ability for these natural materials to breathe allows them to dry out and not hold water. Cob helps to reduce humidity in your building. As it breathes in the air from outside the tiny clay particles soak up the humidity reducing the percentage of water in the air by the time it reaches the interior. The same effect happens when you take a hot shower inside a cob walled bathroom. The cob walls are constantly breathing air in and out, at a rate of about 1" to 2" per hour.

*Here is an example of a partially finished building with no protection from the snow.
When the snow melted the building was unharmed.*

*Snow and rain are not a factor in using cob or straw bale
if you have a good hat and boots*

Myth: If I build with cob or straw my house will look dirty, dusty and like a hobbit house.

Fact: If you would like to build a hobbit house you surely can! But you can also build a fully functionable "modern" looking home out of natural materials. There are homes built and being built as you are reading this all over the world that are over 4000 sq. ft. As I write, I am putting the finishing touches on the interior of my two-story 2200 sq. ft home in Northeast Texas. Also, several of my students across the United States are working on their own homes, ranging from 900 sq. ft to a whopping 4430 sq. ft! My home is fully functional with electricity, water, gas and a huge rocket mass heater with a warming bench. It has three bedrooms, two bathrooms, oak flooring and a custom-built kitchen. Building with natural materials does not limit you, it makes the possibilities limitless.

A beautiful cob island and earthen floor in Ken Jordan's home

Nothing dirty looking in Ken's house here.
You can see more pictures of Ken's home on Facebook under the name of Nad Kad.

Myth: I can't build my own home!

Fact: As with anything in life if you go at it with the attitude of "I can't" then you probably won't. Natural building is laborious and slow, but extremely rewarding if you are the type of person that loves to be hands on, is creative and driven. If you have some common sense and patience, you can do it.

Natural building started with the indigenous people thousands of years ago, long before colleges and certifications. These two basic human instincts have been suppressed by modern technology in recent years - **food and shelter**!

I started my build at the age of 54, after fighting a two-year battle with cancer. That I know of to date, there are at least three natural built homes in the US built by 65- 70-year-old women with little or no help. Still, I highly recommend taking a workshop before trying to start a build, as it will save you from mistakes and do overs, as well as saving you money and time. There is an increase in the popularity of natural building, it is best to ensure the workshop is being held by a reputable source and not a one-time workshop looking for free labor to help with their build. There is the risk that these builders may not have the correct knowledge base to help you with your own build. Learn from someone who can supply their lessons learned from having gone through the process already.

Here I am with my husband Jackie supervising!

Kay has not only built a palletable cob storage shed and a cob oven, but also a 900 square ft bale/cob home that includes a root cellar dug into the side of the mountain. Kay may be in her 60s, but she has the heart and drive of a 20-year-old. Did I mention she did this in a year!?

Myth: You can't get a mortgage or loan on a natural-built home.

Fact: It is possible to get a mortgage, but you may need to search a little more for a lender than with a conventional build. It will be easier to qualify for a loan by doing your plumbing and electrical up to code. This may not mean you have to have inspections and pay for licensed contractors. I bought a book for dummies on how to do electrical by code for my home. When my electrical was finished I had a licensed electrician friend come double check my work to make sure I did it right. I did! Just use common sense if you are planning to try to get a loan against your home.

Myth: I have allergies and a cob house would aggravate them.

Fact: Surprisingly enough, a cob home would help someone suffering from allergies. The breathability of the cob walls removes toxins from the air as it passes slowly through the walls. Not only do the walls naturally clean and filter the air, but you are also living in a natural non-toxic environment, free of chemicals like formaldehyde found in conventional builds. The clay also inhibits mold growth.

Myth: Building with cob would mean that I could only build a small house and couldn't go more than one story.

Fact: Any internet search on Cob is most likely to return images of small Hobbit style cottages. Although these are cute and can be functional for one person, they are not quite what a couple or small family may be looking to live in. Sometimes it is more functional and takes up a smaller footprint to just go up another level to create more square footage

Taos Pueblo in New Mexico contains multi-story structures. In Yemen there are over nine story high cob buildings being used that date back hundreds of years. So to debunk this myth, yes you can have a natural build two stories or more.

Shibam, originally settled 1700 years ago.
City known as the "Manhattan of the Desert"

Myth: I can't have modern comforts in a natural built home - running water, flushing toilets, dishwasher, internet, cable, etc.

Fact: A natural build has no impact on the modern amenities you can have in comparison to a conventional build. Once you have plastered your walls, most people wouldn't even know that your walls are cob or straw.

As you can see just because it is natural
doesn't mean it can't be modern and beautiful.
This is also in Ken Jordan's home.

Myth: My home must be designed by a licensed architect/engineer.

Fact: If you have done your due diligence and bought a property in an area that doesn't require permits and inspections for code, then you can and should design your own home. It is your home and should be exactly the way you want it! If you need advice on roofing or other structural aspects, you can reach out to your workshop instructor. If you have property in an area that requires code inspections and permits you will need to reach out to your local code enforcement office to find out what is required for you to be approved.

Some advice on dealing with the code office: most people have no clue what cob is, when you approach them use the word adobe instead, it is the same material, and they won't be at once defensive because they have never heard of cob. Also, be incredibly careful that you are not in an area with HOA's, as this will be almost impossible to deal with.

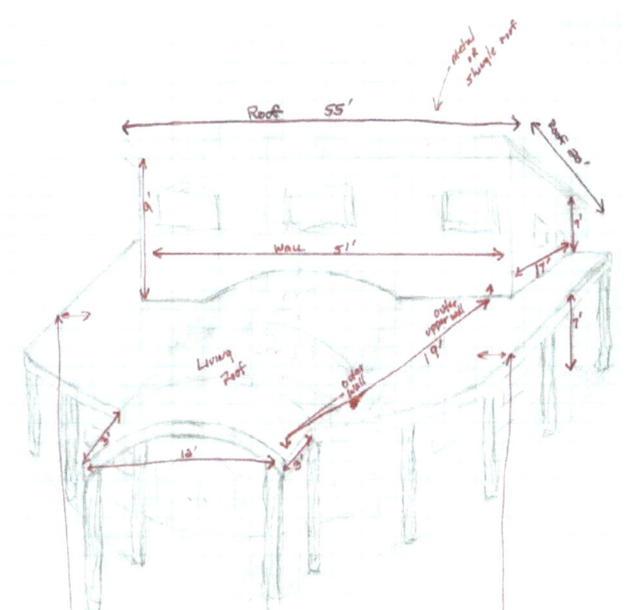

The original design I used to build my house; no architect needed here.

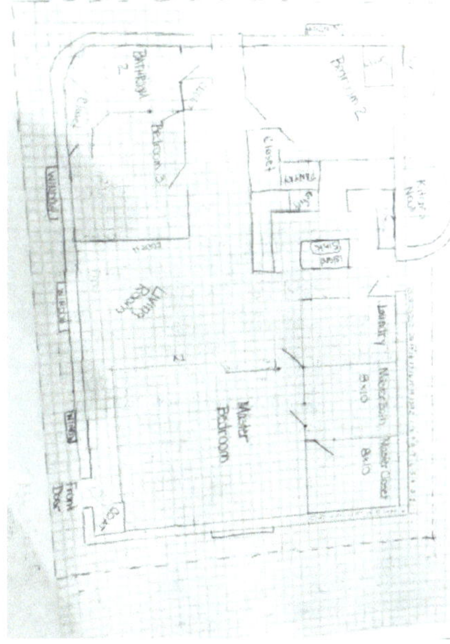

Floor plan hand drawn by owner on graph paper.

Myth: Natural building is a fast way to build my house.

Fact: As much as I would like to tell you that building your own cob/straw bale/cordwood home would be a quick project, it is NOT. Nothing good comes easy, and natural building is the perfect example. Most people only have one or two helpers available, if any, and sourcing your materials and building by hand takes a lot longer than getting ready to install items bought from a big box store.

Example: If you are sourcing the logs for your roof joists from your property you will have to find, cut down, de-limb, and peel them before using. This takes time. The best advice I can give you on this subject is not to give yourself a deadline, but instead a "goal" date. Keep the building process fun and non-stressful by having a comfortable place to stay while building. If you have unrealistic expectations, the build will not be fun and you will be stressed, overworked and could burn out.

That being said, it depends on what style you choose to build with, available resources, and most importantly how much time you put into it. It took nine months of twelve-hour days to get my 2200 sq. ft home to the "ready for interior finishes" stage. I worked so hard I burnt myself out and took three months off. If you don't build as big or build small and add a room at a time. It will make it easier on you. This is an extremely easy medium to add on to, and you can even put up the larger final roof and add on under it. Take your time and have fun!

Audrey definitely knows how to have fun in the mud!

You are never too young to help with cobbing.

Myth: Building with straw will create a fire hazard.

Fact: Straw by itself will burn very easily and quickly!
Fortunately, once straw is covered in clay or cob, it is fireproof. Clay just gets
harder when it is fired in a kiln. So, your cob home, or clay-plastered straw home
is fireproof.

Myth: A natural-built home won't last as long as modern construction.

Fact: The average life expectancy of a modern-day home is 7-10 years, with a
30-year mortgage! The average life expectancy of a natural build—cob, for
example--is 700 years, usually with little to no mortgage. The oldest known
natural build house is thousands of years old and is in Scotland at Knap of Howar
in the Orkney Islands. It is thought to have been built around 3500 BC. So, if you
want to leave a real legacy for your children, grand-children, great-grand-
children….

*The oldest known natural build at
Knap of Howar in Orkney Islands,
Scotland*

*An English cob house
built in 1762.*

Myth: I can build a cob cottage for $500.

Fact: If you built a small cob cottage, let's say a 14-foot circle, you could possibly do that. Of course, it would have no windows, electricity, or running water.

Let's assume you are sourcing your clay from the property, and it is the perfect mixture, so you do not need to buy sand. Then your only purchase for your cob mix would be straw which in the US averages $7.00 a bale. You would need at least 20 bales to mix the cob for this size of cottage.

For your foundation you will need landscape fabric, perforated drainpipe, drain rock and large rock for your stem wall. You will also need drain rock and vapor barrier for your interior foundation. If you could source cheap used wood and a few windows off the internet that would be awesome! For your wood you will need joists and sheathing. Hopefully you can cut and peel some trees off your own property for joists, you will need a pond liner for the living roof (or metal) your choice. So, let's see where we are so far....

Estimated cost for 220 sq. ft with loft:	
Landscape fabric	**$50**
Drain Rock for trench & interior	**$400**
Perforated pipe	**$100**
Stem Wall rock	**$800 (if not free on property)**
Straw	**$140**
Log joists sourced from property (free)OR Dimensional from store	**$300**
Sheathing (plywood)	**$200**
Vapor barrier for foundation	**$17**
Pond liner for living roof or metal	**$380**
Total	**$2387**
NOTE: Prices vary by region (2021 prices)	

So, you can see, we have not even begun to venture into plumbing, electric or appliances. Overall, it is less expensive to build yourself, but just because it is natural doesn't mean it is cheap, so do not be misled! The wonderful thing about it is that if you are building yourself each phase takes a while, and this gives you the opportunity to buy as you build, instead of trying to come up with enormous amounts of money at a time.

Myth: Once I start my build, I can't change the design.

Fact: The absolute best part of natural building is not having to follow some technical, confusing, boring diagram or instructions! Even if you have drawn out a picture and plans for your build, you can easily change, add, or take away as you go! Most builds begin with the footprint (outside walls) and everything else just happens as you get to it, hence "natural" building. A lot of times the ideas you had on paper don't feel as cohesive once you are standing inside. I can honestly say that I rearranged my entire interior floor plan once I got my exterior walls up. Then I added arched niches in my cob walls that I had not planned on, but as you are in the space working ideas will hit you. It makes designing and building your home even more fun!

Myth: I can just search online and join social media groups to get advice on my build.

Fact: Please be cautious in accepting advice, or even "professional" advice on your build. Remember there is no such thing as a true expert, and no substitute for attending workshops. Natural building is different in every climate and region, depending on soil, weather and materials. Make sure you are taking advice from someone who has completed a full build. There are plenty of knowledgeable and reputable natural builders out there that would love to share their knowledge with you. But there are even more that think they know! Do your research!

I can't emphasize this enough, take a workshop and gain the knowledge and experience with hands-on learning to complete your build with confidence. In doing so, you will have a support system and team of knowledgeable builders at your fingertips.

Notes and Sketches

Selecting Your Site

Before you get into details of site selection, let's take a moment and discuss selecting your property. I always urge the students that have signed up for an upcoming workshop to pause their property search until after they complete the workshop.

This spot in the woods is where I finally decided to build my first cob home.

As you can see from this zoomed out perspective, it is quite a large space.

This is why…....

When looking for property to buy for a natural build, the first thing you want to do is check and see what areas do not require permits and inspections. Of course, 99% of the time this will only apply to outside the city limits. Property bought inside any city limits usually has permit/code requirements and a lot of times HOA rules also, so research the areas in which you are thinking about buying land first. Building with permits and code is still doable, but it is going to require way more money because you'll be paying as you go for all your inspections, architects, engineers, licensed electrician, plumbers. It also limits your ability to easily change your plans mid-build.

Assuming you have selected a few properties in an area friendly to natural building, there are some important things to consider as you weigh your options. What follows is a list of such considerations.

Is there water available - a well, pond or stream? You will need water for mixing your cob. Do you have oil/gas rigs or any industry nearby that can be contaminating your water supply for a well?

Are there trees if you plan on harvesting and/or milling your own lumber? If so, what species, and how many?

Is the property in a flood plain? How high is the water table below the property?

Do you see some good build sites on the property? Consider your views and access to light.

These are some of the more important things to consider when looking for property. If you already have property, make sure you know the answers to those questions when selecting the build site on your land. Site selection on your property will vary with your location and region.

When building in the North you want to use the solar gain from the cob, absorbing the heat from the sun and breathing it into the home through the night. In regions that have short summers and long cold winters the goal is to capture as much sun as possible during the day, therefore facing your home to the south would be wise. This would be an area of your home to have windows allowing the sun in for added passive solar gain. The ideal location is then an area on the property that allows the sun to hit the front of the home in the winter. Prime conditions would allow for some trees on the other side to block cold winds.

Note: the winter sun is low enough to heat the walls of the cob when needed.
The higher overhang blocks the sun in the summer keeping the walls cool.

In the Southern areas, where winters are short and mild, the biggest concern is keeping the heat out. This would be carried out by making the south facing overhang of the roof come out further to block the high summer sun from heating up the cob walls. You can also use bale cob in the walls if you want to have more insulation to prevent heat or cold passing through. See discussion on bale/cob later in this book. Another thing to think about when choosing your site is possible solar and water catchment options. If you are planning to have solar then you need to have an open area that will supply maximum solar exposure to your panels.

If planning a water catchment storage area, how will you catch it? Usually, water is caught by a metal roof or a specially designed living roof system. If you are putting in plumbing, plan your area for a septic system also. Make sure that if you are going to be on grid, you have chosen an area on your property that is an affordable distance to run utilities from the road or existing area. Once you have a spot on your property chosen, I highly recommend you camp at that spot and see how it feels. If possible, walk around the area barefoot, feel the earth under your feet, see if that spot feels good to you. How does the sun hit you in the morning as it rises and, in the evening, when it falls? You may find after spending a night there, a spot a little further over has a better view. Don't get in a rush, take your time, see it in the rain and sun. Ideally, experience all four seasons if possible. This may be the spot you spend the rest of your days, so choose accordingly!

A septic system can take up a great deal of space. Keep this in mind when choosing your build site. You do not want your septic anywhere near your water supply.

Installing the septic system can be a team effort and kind of fun.

Make sure you create enough room around your build for any large machinery you may need for placing long, heavy logs or other heavy objects

The most common question people ask when selecting a site is how to determine if they have clay for cob or natural plasters. I know it was for me! In every workshop I have attended, taught or assisted this subject has come up.

Admittedly, when I attended my first workshop, I did not fully understand that we aren't really looking for pure clay. We are just looking for clay rich soil, or soil with some clay in it. Bring a shovel with you and dig down a couple of feet past the topsoil and get a solid sample to check the clay content. If the property has hills, dig closer to the valleys or midway down for clay samples.

The only place to find "pure" clay is a ceramic supply store. Unfortunately, even if you are at a workshop, harvesting clay-rich soil there doesn't help you determine if yours is okay for building. Let me put your fears to rest! Clay is everywhere! There are areas you will have a tough time finding clay--like in bedrock areas or high in the mountains, but you are more likely to have clay in your soil than not! The most common mistake is getting a scoop off the ground, testing it, and being disappointed you can't find clay! Depending on your region, the first couple feet, or sometimes up to four feet, is just organic topsoil. You need to dig down deep enough to see a change in the color and texture of the ground. One tell-tale sign is when the ground where your shovel scrapes shines.

Once you are past the topsoil layer you can collect some samples to test. There are several ways to test your soil for clay. They all work, and it is just a matter of preference. Initially, I was told about the jar test, putting a soil sample in a mason jar of water, shaking it up and reading the results to figure out your percentage of clay. I, like a lot of people, found this way of testing to be not only hard to decide, but left me feeling even more unsure of myself than before. It was extremely difficult to tell from the separations in my jar.

Next, I tried the worm test, wetting a handful of soil and working it into a worm by rubbing my hands together. If I could hang most of it off my hand without it breaking off, I had clay. There is also a drop test, and many more.

But honestly, after all the stress about whether I had clay or trying to figure out how much clay was in my soil, I finally learned it doesn't matter. It doesn't matter how much clay you have if you do have it in your soil. I also learned that the simplest way to know this, is to play with it. Grab a chunk, get it wet, mold it around in your hands, shape it. After you have played with it for a few minutes, roll it into a ball. Is it holding its form? Is it sticky? But most importantly did it leave a slimy layer of whatever color it is on your hands? If your hands are now the same color as the ball you just made, then congratulations, you have clay in your soil! Yes, it is really that easy. There is no perfect ratio. This is *natural* building. This is why "roughly right'" works so well. Finding out the percentage of clay in your soil is about trying to figure out how much sand you may need to add to it to make cob or adobe.

Clay soil rolled into a ball

The easiest and most efficient way to figure out this is to make test cookies. This is amazingly simple. Just make sure they are all the same shape and size. Find a small container you can use to measure consistent amounts. Fill your container with your soil. This will be your first cookie. Mix the first container with water and shape it into a cookie (like a hamburger patty). Next fill your container half full of soil and half full of sand and again mix with water, making the same size cookie. This time draw a line down the center and put the number 1 on each side of it (1|1).

This will tell you that cookie is a one-to-one mix, one part clay soil and one part sand. Continue this by making one part clay, two-part sand and vice versa. The prime place to set your cookies would be on a piece of wood, this helps draw the moisture out from the bottom. Set them in a dry spot preferably in the sun. After a day or two turn them over to allow both sides to dry completely.

When your cookies are completely dry you are ready to test them. Be incredibly careful when biting into them ……. No, I'm kidding, don't eat them :)

It is especially important that this part is done by one person only, because the same person needs to feel the breaking point of each cookie to decide which one was the strongest. Start by looking at all your cookies. Which ones have a lot of cracking? Pick up the first one, does it feel solid or crumbly? Hold it in both hands and try to snap it in half. Did it have a lot of resistance, or did it just fall apart? Now go down the line of cookies repeating that test. When you are done, decide which one was the strongest and that will be your mix. For example, if the cookie that had one part clay and one part sand was the strongest then your cob mix will be 50% clay soil and 50% sand. In a nutshell, you are looking for the one that gave you the most resistance when you tried to break it in half.

Make sure your cookies are all the same size and thickness.

Some parts of the United States have areas of what is referred to as "ready mix". These areas of clay pockets are the perfect mix ratio of sand and clay for building. In this case you just add straw and water, mix and use. When I bought my property in Northeast Texas, I discovered this entire area and all up through Southeast Arkansas is ready-mix. There are people that question whether or not to add sand, since there is already sand and aggregate in the clay soil, not pure clay powder harvested straight from the ground. I agree with this logic. Cob building has been going on since before Christ, so I am sure they dug down and used the clay soil that was available to them. I just can't see them running to the local gravel and sand supplier to buy a load of sand back then.

You can tell when you start working with it if more sand is needed. Make some small batches and test it. In the mix to which you don't add sand, you may want to increase the strength by adding more straw. It only needs to be 'roughly right' to work for you so don't feel pressured into creating a perfect mix ratio. You will read that a perfect cob mix is one part clay and three parts sand. This is true, but you are using rough harvested clay soil not pure store bought clay mix. Performing the cookie test enables you to get as close to that ratio as possible.

Clay comes in many colors. The area you are in will decide the color of your clay soil. Happily, I ended up with the beautiful red clay found here in Northeast Texas. Don't panic if your clay soil is not a desired color, your finish plaster coat can be any color you choose.

If you are going to buy sand for your mix, do not buy "play-sand" or "beach sand." This is the sand sold at the big box stores and is tiny round pebbles that have been smoothed by the many years of water running over them. You want "construction sand" this is the sand they sell at the sand and gravel supply companies used for concrete mix. This sand mix is the crumbs from rock crushing. It consists of tiny, rough-shaped rocks that when compacted together lock in place instead of rolling over each other. Now that you know the basics of how to find clay soil and figure out what mix is right for you, take off your adult hat, put on your kid hat and go play in the mud!

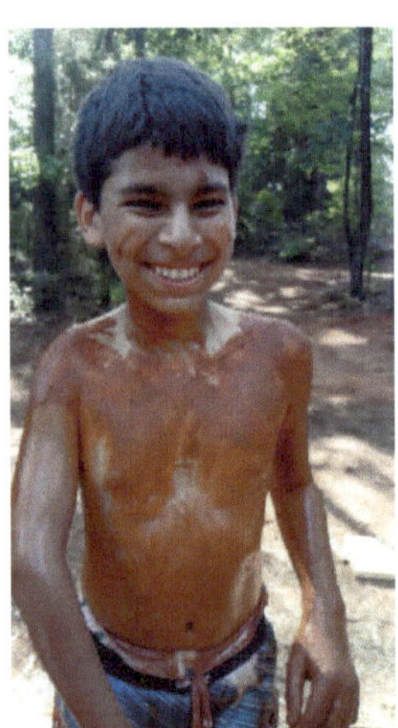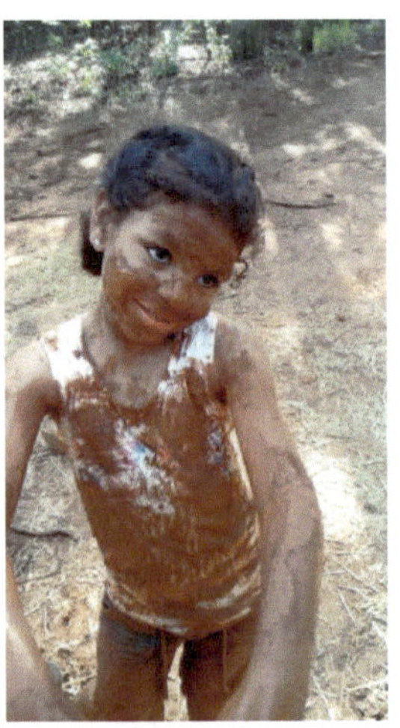

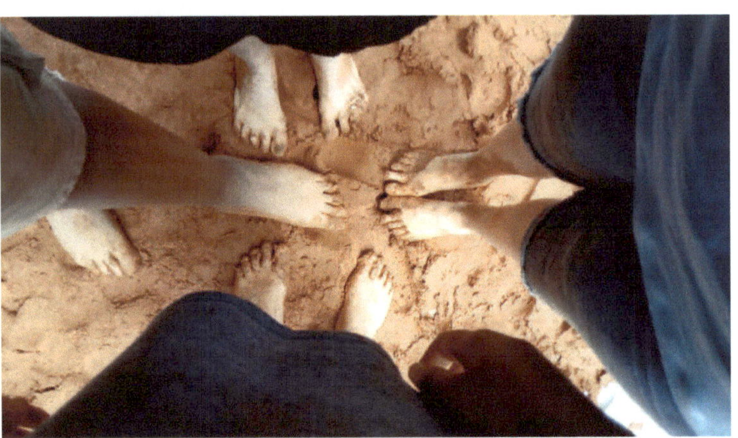

Common Mistakes with Site Selection

- One of the most common mistakes made choosing a spot to build your home is finding the most beautiful spot and putting it there. You just destroyed that pretty spot on your property. Instead look for the ugliest spot and make it beautiful with your home! Even better if it is positioned to view the prettiest spot!

- Do not build your home at the bottom of a hill or slope, unless you have prepared the landscape to deal with all the runoff water that would flow towards your home. Make sure that the location you choose has given you enough room for any heavy equipment to access around it. This is important when it comes time to position long roofing lumber, installing utilities such as electric, water or septic. You may get lucky and find someone with a tractor that can help.

- Be careful not to go in and wipe out every tree around the area. Only take down the ones you are sure need to go. If in doubt, wait until they are in the way, you will be glad you didn't take down so many in the summer.

Notes and Sketches

The Many Styles of Natural Building

Building with natural materials has been used since prehistoric times. It is not something that requires a diploma, degree, or a license. It does however require common sense, patience, creativity, persistence and hard work. The reward for this work feels so good and empowering I cannot possibly find words to describe it. You must experience it for yourself. Because it has been around so long, and is so flexible and forgiving, people have developed unique styles of using the natural materials they have available in their area. Another huge factor on how you build will be created is the weather conditions of your area.

This chapter in no way covers every conceivable way to build your home, but it does cover the more common styles used here in the US.

Cob

Cob is the oldest and the most original style of building; it is done by mixing together clay soil, sand, straw and water. The mix is then placed on a stem wall and rubble trench and kneaded together to create a wall. Depending on the height of the cob wall it can be anywhere from over 18" to 48" wide at the base. The cob does not need any support beams and can hold a massive amount of weight. I personally was absolutely amazed at the strength of dried cob the first time I tried to trim some off a wall. Mixing the cob is probably the simplest part of learning natural building, however the labor involved will definitely get you in shape! The straw mixed into the mix of clay soil and sand gives the mix a tensile strength similar to the rebar in a concrete slab. When you are applying the cob to the wall, you are in fact sewing the pieces of straw from the lump you are applying to the existing cob on the wall. Just reading about the cob application and the correct mix was not enough to give me confidence to start building. Getting my hands in it and feeling it gave me all the confidence I needed. Clay comes in many colors, depending on the region you are in. I have pockets or veins of yellow clay in spots here on my property even though the majority is red. The color isn't going to change the cob mix, unless you are just getting a lot of silt or organic matter and not clay. Remember you can always plaster with a different color clay for your final coat if you don't care for your cob color.

Below you can see a beautiful cob home built by a couple that came through one of my workshops last year. They left here, drove to their property in

Colorado and immediately proceeded to start their build. They did a great job, it makes all the difference having that hands-on knowledge and confidence!

This build was done by mixing all the cob on tarps,with their feet. They did not have tractors to mix the cob. The cob itself can be a gorgeous finish, and a lot of people prefer to leave the cob look on the exterior instead of plastering. This is fine. Because if you have done a good job on your boots and hat, your walls will last just as long and look great! Each mix of cob is not going to be exactly the same, because you can't control what is in each scoop of clay mixed soil. This is again where the term "roughly right" comes in. The mix doesn't have to be perfect every time, roughly right works! The important things to remember when cobbling is keeping your walls plumb and trimmed, and not adding on too much height at one time without allowing for dry time.

If your mix is too wet add a little more dry material. Too dry? Add water. It is ridiculously simple to master the cob, and very fun to play in!

So proud of students Emma and Clayton who went straight from a workshop to starting their build in Colorado.

Even in the snow this home looks cozy and warm

*Making cob balls is a fun time
to strike up conversation!*

*Teaming up with someone on the interior
and exterior while cobbing helps to keep
the walls going up evenly*

Cob soil is a natural anti-depressant. Yes it's true! It contains a substance called *Mycobacterium vaccae*. This has been found to trigger the effects of neurons that drugs like Prozac provide. The bacterium may also stimulate serotonin production making you more relaxed and happy. This is why it has been such a successful material to use with our PTSD veterans and everyone else attending our workshops. Jump in and be happy!

Enjoying the benefits of "My Cob Vacay!"

Bale/Cob

In areas and regions where more insulation is a need due to severe heat or cold, straw bale and cob are an excellent choice. The build is started the same as cob, with a rubble trench and stem wall. Then a layer of cob is placed on the stem well to level the top. Once the entire stem wall is leveled with a layer of cob, straw bales are stacked down the center, brick style with wood stakes holding them in place. Cob is then added to the inside and outside walls of straw. Bales can be cut long ways to make them thinner if desired. This can be done on North walls, or on any of the walls. This is dependent on the desired insulation needed.

Bale/cob style building is very insulative against severe hot or cold climates. Straw bales are covered with cob on exterior and interior.

Straw bales are stacked and speared with wooden stakes in a brick style pattern. This prevents running seams. NOTE: A final layer of cob along the top of the walls gives you weight to compress the bales and a place to attach the roof joists.

Straw Bale

There are so many ways to build with straw bales, we will not get into the details. That is a whole separate book! If you are wanting to learn more about straw bale building, I highly recommend reading Athena Steen's book - The Straw Bale House (Real Goods Independent Living Book).

The most common way straw bales are used is as an infill between the wood framed exterior walls. Straw bales can also be load bearing on their own, although they need to be compressed before you try to plaster. The foundation can still be rubble trench and stem wall, although lately they are using concrete foundations for the bigger homes that are being contracted out to big builders.

Framing ready to infill with straw bales (built by Ken Jordan)

Ken Jordan's walls filled with straw bales and ready for plaster

Once plastered, straw bale homes are thick, smooth and appealing to the eyes

Light Clay Straw

If you have unlimited access to cheap straw, and not an abundance of clay soil and sand, this is a practical choice. This is also a great method of insulating or retrofitting an already existing building.

Clay is mixed with water to create a thin gravy consistency; this is called clay slip. The clay slip is dribbled over a tarp with loose straw piled onto it. The straw is "tossed" like a salad, until all the straw is coated lightly in slip. The coated straw is then placed between the 2 x 4's or other wood framing in the walls, A piece of plywood is temporarily screwed to the wall, starting at the bottom and working your way up to the ceiling. As you add the slipped straw into the form it is compacted down into the wall, as you work up the wall, your plywood is unscrewed and moved up. This creates a perfectly insulated space in your walls that is ready for plater, sheathing or even sheetrock if you want.

Plywood forms are screwed to framing and straw tossed in clay slip is rammed into the wall. This process continues upward until the framing is filled, resulting in well insulated walls.

Above and below: These wood frames are being formed and filled with light clay straw to create prefabbed walls that will be added to a build. These sections pictured here will be placed on top of an eight-foot-tall cob wall forming the top section of a lighthouse themed build in Bandon, Oregon at Sustainable U.

Adobe

Unbelievably, adobe and cob are the same thing. The word cob means lump or loaf, the word adobe means brick form or clay brick. Adobe is essentially dried cob, but does not require the same amount of straw. Some adobe bricks don't have any straw. The mix is smashed into brick forms and left to dry in the sun, creating a clay brick called adobe. These bricks are then used to construct the walls of the house, using cob as the mortar. Adobe walls are then coated with natural clay plasters. Using adobe bricks can help to keep the walls more square and uniform, also making arched doorways and windows steadier and easier to create.

Adobe wall mortared with cob

Adobe bricks are made by mixing clay, sand, straw and water and putting the mix in wooden brick shaped forms. The forms are then removed, and the bricks are left to dry in the sun. Adobe bricks are not fired in a kiln

As the wall is completed, natural clay plaster is applied to the adobe bricks.

Rammed Earth

Just like it sounds, clay soil mix is rammed into pre-built wooden forms. This is probably the most expensive method due to the labor involved. The clay soil also must be ideal. If this method is used in an environment subject to extreme heat or cold, added insulation will be needed as there is no insulative value in the rammed earth walls. The walls have beautiful layers of clay colors when completed, making the end results highly sought after.

Church of the Holy Cross in Stateburg South Carolina, built 1850 - 1852 created with rammed earth and designed by Edward C Jones. This was marked as a historical landmark in 1973

This is the Jiayuguan Wall (The Great Wall of China). Construction began in 1372, and this is the largest known rammed earth project in history

Cordwood

This is a type of build that requires some pre-planning and early preparation work. The pre-cut to size pieces of wood, usually short logs, need to be "seasoned" or allowed to fully dry and shrink prior to use. Once they are ready, they are mortared together over the stem wall/foundation creating a thick beautiful wall of round wooden shapes embedded in the mortar.

Richard Flatau has been building cordwood homes for over 40 years. Below are some images showing the process for a cordwood build. I would encourage you to visit his website https://cordwoodconstruction.org/ for images of completed builds.

This cedar Eden cabin located in New York was built by Tom Huber who was A master cordwood builder (photo provided by Richard Flatau). Note the strategically placed bottle bricks let light through the wall.

This home in South Korea is not only made with cordwood but also with cob, making it a cob-wood home. Picture courtesy of Richard Flatau.

Palletable Cob

This is a newer version of natural building introduced and made popular by Miguel Elliott after turning a tented homeless encampment under an Oakland California Freeway into a gorgeous Cob Village, used pallets are attached together between support posts to create the outside frame of the home. The pallets are then stuffed with straw. Stuffed pallets are cobbed on the inside and outside creating a beautiful insulated strong wall. This method not only speeds up the building process but uses recycled materials!

All you need are pallets and straw! Pallets are attached to vertical posts to create a wall. Straw is stuffed inside, and cob is used to cover the interior and exterior.

*Palletable cobin ready for cob. This was built by Miguel Elliott,
also known as "Sir Cobalot"*

*As you can see above, using pallets does not restrict you from being creative.
This is another wonderful creation by Miguel Elliott*

Timber Frame

This method involves framing out your build with either logs or dimensional lumber. Once the framing is complete it can be infilled with any material from straw, cob, hemp, light clay straw, etc.

There are several great books on timber framing with both dimensional lumber as well as round logs. I recommend The Natural Building Companion Jacob Deva Racusin and Ace McAreleton. Will Beemer's <u>Learn to Timber Frame</u> is also a reputable resource.

Above is a timber frame build ready for the walls to be infilled with straw bales.

Raising a round timber support for the roofing structure

Common Mistakes when Selecting a Style

- Most people I have talked to wished they had been aware of the many building style options before they started their build.

- Failing to research the style that would be best for you can cost you so much time, money and frustration

- Upon finishing your rubble trench your build size will look smaller than it really is. A huge mistake often made by first time builders is panicking and adding more square footage at this stage. This results in more costs, labor and time.

- Another mistake often made is choosing a style that requires materials you do not have readily available on your property.

Notes and Sketches

Good boots —The Foundation

As with anything, if the foundation is not solid and secure then neither will be anything built upon it. There are variations of how the stem wall and rubble trench can be designed, as different building styles may require a slightly distinctive design.

When building with cob or bale/cob a rubble trench and stem wall can be built taller in areas of sideways driving rain and smaller roof overhangs. This gives the lower parts of your exterior walls more protection from the elements and keeps your cob areas safer. The stem wall is built on a rubble trench. A rubble trench is remarkably like a French drain, in fact it pretty much is a French drain on steroids! The rubble trench not only directs water away from your build, but also supplies a solid foundation for your walls.

The gravel in the rubble trench allows your entire home the ability to move as one solid monolithic object, making your home earthquake proof up to a 10.1 earthquake. The rubble trench is dug to a depth that is below the freeze line, the depth of which varies from region to region. The trench should not be less than 18" deep to ensure enough room for drainpipe and drain rock. The width of the trench depends on the desired thickness of the base of the walls. The higher the walls, the thicker the base needs to be. On average the trench is usually 18" to 24" wide.

The trench is lined with landscape fabric to keep the dirt from clogging it up. Inside the fabric a perforated drainpipe is added to help the water run out faster. The trench is then filled with drain rock folding the landscape fabric over the top creating a "burrito".

Once the trench is dug it is ready for landscape fabric. As you can see it runs downhill away from the build rerouting any water away from your walls.

The landscape fabric has been laid and is now ready for the perforated pipe.

The pipe is then covered with drain rock.

The drain rock does not reach the top of the trench. It stops about 3" below the top.

Fold over the landscape material, burrito style.

It is then ready for the stem wall on top. Often the stem wall rock is stacked in such a way as to rise higher at each side of the front entrance of the home. This naturally frames out and creates a "grand" entrance. This also gives your finished walls a very artistic and appealing look.

There are several ways to build the stem walls. The oldest and most proven method is dry stacking. Dry stacking uses small 1" or smaller granite rocks, referred to as "heartening" or "fines" between every layer of stem wall rock to not only create a stable surface, but to cause the stem wall rock to "lock" together. The "fines" are not smooth, but jagged pieces that when compressed lock together and cannot move or slide. Another more modern way of securing a stem wall is mortar. Mortar can be made from cement or from lime. Obviously, lime would be the preferred choice as it is on the "natural" spectrum.

Dry stacking is the art of creating or building a wall using stone without a mortar in between the layers. In the above photo you can see them stacking without using the small heartening stone. The heartening serves many purposes such as helping large rocks lock together, supplying a smoother surface between layers and filling in all the gaps between the rocks thus deterring critters from finding a home. The rocks being used in the above photo are volcanic, very coarse and rough, and they lock together easily. The gaps will be lime pointed when complete.

In the pictures below, you can see how the heartening has filled in the gaps and prepared the wall for the next layer of rock. Also notice the pipes laid into the ground layer preparing the space for utilities to run through.

If you are planning to build a timber frame on your stem wall for straw bale, light straw clay, cordwood or just wood, you would want to have either all thread rods, rebar or wooden stakes protruding out the top of your stem wall to secure your wood frame base too. This keeps your walls from sliding out of place while building. Also, having a level surface at the top is important for this style.

All thread

Rebar

When preparing for bale/cob you can use cob to create a level surface for straw bales. In doing so you can add wooden stakes directly into your stem wall and first layer of cob to hold your first level of bales in place.

Stakes

Above you can see the process of applying a level layer of cob on the stem wall to prepare for the installation of straw bales. Also note that Luke has figured out that clay slip makes for a good sunscreen and mosquito repellant!

If you are in an area with no access to large rocks to use for a stem wall, there are some "free source" options. The most common alternative to using rocks is urbanite. Urbanite is medium to generous sized chunks of broken concrete. When I say large, I am referring to a size still small enough to man-handle with two people. Using urbanite not only gives you an opportunity to acquire low cost or free building materials, but also the opportunity to recycle/repurpose.

Some other low cost or free options could be used cinder urbanite, blocks, or bricks.

Keep in mind when you choose the dimensional shapes, it will require more work and a more precise application to keep a level uniform look. Another possibility, not on the inexpensive, or "natural" spectrum, would be a concrete poured footer using a form. When choosing your stem wall rock, it needs to be non-absorbing. Do not use sandstone or a material that will defeat the purpose of your stem wall by wicking ground moisture up into your walls.

When your stem wall is complete you can use a lime mortar to "point" between your rock or stem wall material (that is, if you did not use mortar or heartening). Lime pointing fills in any possible air gaps, preventing drafts, moisture and little critters from entering the home. In my opinion it also gives it a very finished and clean look.

The stem wall material can be rock or urbanite (broken concrete). The rock again, needs to be hard, no sandstone or rock, this would wick up the moisture to the cob walls. Other materials that can be used for the stem wall are bricks, cinder blocks, or if preferred, a poured concrete form.

The interior foundation, after being leveled, will consist of three layers. The first layer will be the vapor barrier, second 4" of drain rock, and the third will be another 4" of tamped flex base. If you are building in the north with a severe cold climate, you will have four layers, beginning with an insulation layer. Usually consisting of a 2" closed cell foam.

*This is an example of applying your vapor barrier, drain rock, and final tamped layer of flex base.
Note that your actual datum (final floor height) will depend on
what material you add as your final floor.*

Miguel Elliott laying an earthen floor in his palletable cobin. The topic of earthen floors is worthy of more discussion than we can offer here. A book that offers a nice breakdown on this topic is <u>Building with Cob—a Step by Step Guide</u> by Adam Weismann and Katy Bryce.

Common Mistakes with Foundations

- Forgetting to run plumbing before stem wall
- Building a stem wall with no rubble trench
- Not leveling your site before digging the trench
- Filling the trench with material that won't allow drainage
- Putting posts in the rubble trench blocking it
- Not using landscape fabric
- Not digging an exit for rubble trench
- Not building a stem wall, cob on the ground
- Using cob as mortar on the stem wall
- Using sandstone on stem wall

Notes and Sketches

The Walls

Once you have completed your foundation and stem wall, you are ready to begin going vertical with your walls. There are a couple of things to keep in mind before you just jump in and start going up.

Do you need to have any cables coming in, such as electrical, satellite, gas? Most of the main utilities will go through the base of your stem wall, but if they were forgotten or you want them run above ground, now is the time to plan for them. You can easily lay a piece of PVC pipe across your walls at any height to allow access to run lines through later. If you choose not to use it, cob it in. Also, it saves time to plan your electrical outlets, switches and running wires as you work your way up the interior. This saves you having to go back and dig them in later.

Depending on the style of build you have decided on, the walls can be the longest of the building process. Even with several people working, there is only so high you can go with cob until it needs some drying time. This is usually a day or two, depending on your weather conditions. It is not necessarily a terrible thing for the walls to be a longer process. This is the part of the build that makes it yours. The walls are a blank canvas waiting to be sculpted into your custom art piece!

This niche was not in my plans, it was something I decided to add on as I built up my wall.

This has so much creativity going on. Besides the well-sculpted Buddha, see the way the cob appears to be dripping down the walls like frosting on a cake.

These faces were done by Mike Droske. I can tell you I may have nightmares waking up to these in the night, but still very well done, Mike!

Bottle bricks, shelves and a bench! Wow!

We put a spare piece of glass in a wooden window buck creating an artistic opportunity for our students. They nailed it!

So much talent and creativity! Willow and Sylvia definitely rocked this one.

This is the stage where you add all the custom, unique and personal touches to your dream home! This can consist of simple, soft lines, sculpting three dimensional designs, or creating a beautiful mosaic with the filtered light from a wall of colored bottle bricks! Take your time, have fun with it! We did in the above pictures!

If you are building with cob, you will work around the entire stem wall a layer at a time. You never cob in 'sections'. This creates 'shear points' or seams in your walls, the strength of a cob wall comes from its ability to be one monolithic piece, not separate pieces.

Notice how the stem wall is completely covered in the first layer before moving upward.
This keeps the strengths as one monolithic piece instead of sections creating weak seams.

For a good strong cob build, the outside wall should have a slight slant inward. This creates a wide 'foot' base giving the wall extra strength and stability. A common slant is a 1/2" per foot going up. This can vary depending on the height and thickness of your base. The top of the wall should never end up less than a foot thick.

You never want to end up with less than a foot in width at the top of your tapered wall. Either tape less per foot or create a wider base. The wider base is a better choice. Remember the interior wall is not tapered.

*Above is an easy "hack" to achieve this slant using a four-foot level and a
cut piece of 2" x 4" wood. (See tool section)*

Make sure you are keeping your walls plumb as you cob. Never cob
higher than one foot without stopping to plumb and trim. Never leave the build for
the day without plumbing up the walls and trimming. When coming back later to
continue cobbing your cob may already be dry. Never add cob to a dry surface, it
will not stick. When adding cob to dry cob you will need to wet your dry surface
first. The rule of thumb is cob to cob is always just water, cob to any other
material like wood, burlap, rock, etc. you will always use clay slip. Clay slip is clay
watered down to a gravy consistency.

Cat using a cob saw to show how to correctly plumb a cob wall.

Kristen has mastered the use of the tapered level for plumbing the cob wall exterior.

Applying clay slip to straw to prepare it for cob.

Application of clay slip on "porcupined" door and window bucks.

The slip should cover your hand like a glove.

Wet cob is extremely heavy! When you get lop-sided on your wall, and all the weight is pulling to one side, you will end up with a messy and sometimes dangerous "cobalanche," especially when your cob is wet, and you are going up in height too fast. As a result, you just tripled your workload with cleanup and recobbing that wall section.

Another thing that helps keep the walls going up at a more even plumb rate is to cob in teams of two. This means one person on the inside, one on the outside, working in tandem as you go along the wall. Doing this prevents one side getting heavier than the other. Even with this style you will still check your plumb every foot you go up.

As you cob your way up in height there are several things to remember. Take your time, don't get caught up in the excitement of the wall going up and forget things like a planned window or door opening. Unbelievably, this is easy to do, especially when you have multiple people working on a wall.

As you add your doors, window bucks and deadmen into your walls, they will require porcupines, that is, a lot of nails on the cob facing sides of the wood. The photo below shows a porcupine being added to a window back to strengthen the structure. Porcupines are placed on the bottom, middle and top sides of all doors and large windows. On small to mid-sized windows, it usually only requires one at the top side and one on bottom. This gives you a sturdy piece to attach your buck to, preventing future movement from constant opening and closing of doors and windows.

*In this pic you can see the side of the door buck has already been
screwed to a porcupine which will be cobbed into the wall giving
the door buck much needed support and stability.
The buck itself can then be "porcupined."*

The deadmen on the other hand are pieces of wood, nailed on the back
and sides embedded into the cob wall on the interior side. These are placed in
areas you know require heavy items to be hung on the wall later. Such as
cabinets, big screen TVs, shelves or paintings. If in doubt, put a deadman there,
it will be plastered over anyway. This gives you a sturdy piece to attach your
buck to, preventing future movement from constant opening and closing of doors
and windows.

If you have decided on bale/cob for your build you will cob on the top of your stem wall to level it. This creates a level surface to place your straw bales. The thickness can vary from a few inches to a foot depending on what is needed to get it level. Remember to level It not only from right to left, but also inside to outside. Also, if your build is not round and has corners it is wise to keep the corners solid cob all the way up creating a strong buttress with no shear spot.

Cob up all the way also around doorways for stability, as this makes the doorway stable and strong. The straw bales should be stacked in a brick style to prevent any running seams. As you work your way up, each straw bale should be staked to the ones below using wooden stakes. You can make these by gathering strong 1" or so thick branches and making a point on one end with a machete. The length is not as important as long as it goes through both bales.

It takes teamwork to push the bales together at the same time you are staking them down. Also notice the outgoing septic has already been run through the wall to connect to later.

Using the branches from nearby trees you have taken down for creating stakes makes a nice use of otherwise wasted wood.

Ideally you want to cob your bales as you go up in height (interior and exterior). This supplies protection from rain, weather and rodents as you build. If a straw bale gets wet, it must be removed and replaced! Wet straw bales will create a mold situation in your walls!

Your straw bales do not have to be full size bales, you can add two or more strings to a "2 string" bale and cut it in half long ways. This is done using a chainsaw (Note: use an already dull chain, as it will dull a chain quickly). Using half bales keeps your walls at a nice manageable thickness, supplying a great insulative value! Using full bales creates an almost 3-foot-thick wall and requires a lot more rubble trench and stem wall, this would be very expensive, laborious and overkill in most areas of the United States. I know this because that is how I built my bale/cob home.

Kay and Tim cut a straw bale in half with an already dull chain-saw blade.

Timber frame and straw bale styles both require framing out the entire build first. This has many advantages if you can afford the lumber or have access to trees for harvesting. Having the roof up before you start infilling the walls is a huge advantage. With the roof in place, you have the freedom to work on your build in weather you otherwise couldn't, because it supplies protection from the elements. Also, having the walls framed out already, you are just infilling an already plumbed area, this speeds up the process. At this point your walls can be infilled with straw, hemp, cob, light clay straw and more!

Whatever style you decide on, life will be much easier on you if you build your roof system first. This saves you so many miserable hours of repairing and untarping your build.

Imagine having to fight with hundreds of pounds of tarps every time you hear a thunderclap! This is life without a roof first.

Common Mistakes with Walls

- Leaving tarps over walls. If you do not have your roof built before your walls, make sure you have enough tarps to cover the tops and sides of your walls. Make sure they are tied down, so the winds don't blow them away. A common mistake is keeping tarps on a wet build. This will cause mold and condensation. Remove tarps in clear weather.

- Forgetting utilities. Don't forget to run your electric lines on the interior walls as you build upward.

- Running water lines through cob/straw walls. Never run water lines in a cob or straw bale wall. Keep it through the stem wall, floor and interior walls.

- Cobbing all the way down the stem wall. Do not cob over your stem wall on the exterior until your cob is touching the ground. The stem wall is there to keep the cob from wicking up water from the ground.

- Cobbing up too high without checking plumb. Trim and check your plumb every foot of rise.

- Cobbing with a mix that is too wet. If your cob just oozes out instead of holding its shape and gaining height it is too wet. Add more straw and more dry mix as needed.

- Forgetting to add deadmen. Do not be shy about putting deadmen in your walls, you never know where you may want to hang something on a wall later.

- Not keeping track of where you have run water and power lines in walls/floor. I highly recommend that you take lots of pictures of where your water and electrical lines are before you cover them up. Remember this house will last for hundreds of years, unlike today's conventional builds. Make a photo album of step-by-step documentation and instructions for either your children or the next owners that way they know where everything is if they have an issue. This will also come in handy for you later if you can't remember where the electric wire is located within a certain wall, and you are wanting to drive a long nail in it or cut it out for a window.

Notes and Sketches

A Great Hat —The Roof

This stage of the building process seems to be the scariest for first time builders. In all honesty I have to say it was for me too! As I began the roof phase of my build, I had nightmares about the whole thing collapsing on my grandkids while they were visiting! This was the most stressful part of the build for me! As it turned out, once again I was overthinking it! The roof is actually a quite simple step in your build, if you have a little bit of common sense, you will be fine!

If you keep the roof simple in design, it will be easier to figure out! The most common roof designs used in natural buildings are shed style, gable, and reciprocal. The easiest to design and build is the shed roof. This is also the perfect design to use for water catchment. Your joists can be peeled logs that you harvested off your property, or dimensional lumber you buy at a lumber yard. You can even have your logs milled to size if you have a sawmill available for use or hire.

If you are planning to have a metal roof then you would probably have an easier time using dimensional lumber for your roofing material, as the metal requires a smoother, straighter surface. For a living roof you can most definitely use logs, the curves just add character to the roof!

I have been asked if it is possible to use asphalt shingles on a natural building roof. Well yes, but it takes away the "natural." There are many options for the roofing material: metal, shingles, cedar shakes, thatch, living roof (pond liner) and more! The question is what is readily available to you? What do you want to spend? The roof is not a place to get cheap on, or you will be replacing it sooner than later! But if you do the work yourself it doesn't have to break the bank either.

I have found that a metal roof and a quality living roof usually end up costing about the same when it is all said and done, of course I am sure this varies in different areas. I will say that the living roof is my favorite style, with metal being my second choice. The metal roof is a basic construction process that includes joists, sheathing or plywood, felt paper and then the metal.

A metal roof is an excellent choice for water catchment.

A living roof, however, can be a bit more complex depending on your design. We will keep it simple here and save the complex to the seasoned builders for now.

Let's look at the layers of a living roof system, starting with the joists. Let's assume that you can harvest your own logs off your property (or nearby). Before using them, it is particularly important to peel the bark off them, this should be done as soon as possible after harvesting,

The reason the bark is removed is because the beetles that eat away the wood live in the safe space between the bark and the tree. Removing the bark rids the tree of these parasites, not to mention it looks prettier too!

Peeling the bark off the logs using draw knives

Peeled logs ready for application

Kay's home is framed out with round timber.

*If you have high wind concerns you can place porcupine deadmen
into the top plate of cob to screw your logs down to.*

I will now share with you a major and painful lesson learned by me in this process. When you peel trees, there is much sap released from the trees, which can be used to make pitch glue. I made the mistake of sitting on the tree as I worked my way down the log. Focusing on my work, I kept going until I really needed a bathroom break. I rushed into the bathroom, quickly unbuttoning my jeans only to realize they were stuck to my butt! Panicking, I had to forcefully yank down my jeans taking with them the first layer of my skin. Still jumping with the need to pee I sat on the toilet. After relieving myself, sudden dread spread over me, I had now glued myself to the toilet seat. Another layer of skin later, and I still have the scars to prove I made a mistake that will never be repeated! Place cardboard or another protective layer between you and the log when peeling to avoid suffering from "sticky butt."

So now that we have peeled logs to use as joists, we are ready for sheathing. As logs are not squared or perfectly flat, it would be hard to try to use plywood, though not impossible with a lot of shimming here and there, or you can use milled live edge about ½" thick if overlapping or ¾" thick if side by side. You can also try for a free source and re-use old barn wood for this step. Remember this is to support the roof material between the joists. This sheathing will not show, except on the interior ceiling if you leave it bare, so it is okay if the colors differ. They cannot be rotten or weak. When you have your sheathing up you should be able to walk confidently on it without any give under your weight. You should always use screws to attach your sheathing for the living roof, as nails tend to work themselves back out sometimes creating a puncture in your vapor barrier.

Milling sheathing for living roof

Notice the 1/2" live edge sheathing is overlapped for strength on the roof. The log joists are resting on the cob wall and will be infilled with cob later.

The interior view of this style roof is very appealing and does not need covering.

The sheathing for my living roof is done. It took me two months to harvest and mill this by myself.

Now that the sheathing is on, we are ready for the felt paper. This acts not only as a backup vapor barrier but also gives an extra layer of protection between the pond liner and the wood.

The next step is usually where you would put up the pond liner, but I do a bit more first. This is optional but recommended to put a little more cushion between the wood and the pond liner. I add broken down cardboard boxes. Use as much as you want or have! The more cushion between the wood sheathing and the pond liner, the less chance of puncture while walking on it. The cardboard also adds more insulation value to your roof! You can tape it in place to keep it from moving when you add it. Do not puncture the felt paper by stapling it down! The staples can work loose and puncture your liner later. Once you have the cardboard placed, go ahead and add your pond liner.

Adding some facia boards along the roof edge will help hold your earthen substrate and keep it from falling off in heavy storms. Once your facia is up, you can pile on straw, compost, mulch, or whatever you must to create good growing conditions. Most people prefer succulents because they are minimal maintenance, but you can also plant yourself an herb garden on your roof!

A good example of pond liner and facia being added. Note the upstairs shed roof is directing the water towards the uphill side of the build. To correct this guttering will be added to redirect water to the sides.

The pond liner is then covered with a thick layer of straw. In the spring, compost and mulch will be added for growing plants.

The organic layer above the pond liner wraps around my entire roof.

I know the roof seems to be intimidating, but once you have seen the simplicity in the design, and the strength in the correct placement of your joists, it will be a more relaxed and confident phase of the build for you. I have tried to include as many pictures as possible to help you see the options available, but also to see the importance of attending a workshop to acquire the confidence and knowledge you will need to build your roof system with success.

Below is what is called a reciprocal roof system, these are extremely popular with natural builders. These are based on the concept of each log overlapping and locking the next in place. This design is very appealing to the eye and allows for the opportunity of a skylight or cupola in the center if desired.

In a reciprocal roof, the first log is temporarily attached to a "Charlie" pole. This holds it in place as you add the rest of the logs overlapping each other.

When the Charlie pole is removed, the logs in a reciprocal roof stay locked in place and are ready for sheathing. The center will have a cupola built over it later.

As you can see, the use of crooked logs gives the roof a whimsical look.

Common Mistakes with Roofing

- One of the most common mistakes I see in living roof construction is using a plastic drop cloth or tarp for a vapor barrier. These do not block water for long and dry rot or puncture rather quickly. I highly recommend EPDM #45ml liner for roofing a living roof system. It will last a lifetime if covered correctly.

- Another mistake is building the roof to shed water toward the uphill side of the home, directing the flow back to the walls.

- Not building enough overhang to protect the walls. Cob should have a minimum of 2 feet overhang, but 3 is preferred.

- Failure to use roofing felt because you assume it is not natural. Contrary to belief, (asphalt paper) roofing felt, is 100% organic. The felt paper is made with the waste product from the production of asphalt. This waste product is actually the only organic component in the process.

- Do not forget too if you are planning to put solar panels on your roof to have the correct angles facing south.

Notes and Sketches

Windows and Doors

This is an especially important part of your build plan, probably more important than you realize. In a natural build a window location isn't just about seeing outside, just as your door is not just an entrance. Before we get into detail, let's start with the basics.

Your windows and door openings will be previously planned and created as your walls go up, usually by placing window and door bucks for easy installation later.

Door bucks are being put in first since they sit at floor level. Notice the window buck sitting on the first layer of straw, this was one of my first mistakes. I did not factor in my final floor height and had the window sitting way too low. Luckily, I noticed in time and was able to raise it.

You need to be vigilant about bracing these buck frames so they can remain square, level and plumb during the wall building process.

Brace the frame! Make sure your door and window bucks are well braced or they will be out of level and plumb when you are done with your walls.

Bucks can twist and bend easily from the weight of the cob or from pressing straw bales. This makes it exceedingly difficult to install your windows later. If you have not figured out and marked your datum (final floor height) don't forget to add that in the height placement of your window and door bucks. This is one of the many lessons I learned the hard way. Standing inside of your new home before adding your 4" of tamped drain rock, 4" of tamped flex base and the thickness of your flooring material your window can end up being over 8" lower than where you are looking at it right now. My windows would have been below my shoulder height if I had not noticed my mistake before I had gotten any higher with my cob walls.

There is a lot of room to be creative with your window placement. If you want a deep window space for placing items or even creating a bench or reading nook then you can place your window to the outside edge, or if you prefer to have a large sill on the outside then place the window towards the interior more. Keep in mind, the further toward the inside the less passive solar gain you will receive if it is a very thick wall.

The placement of your windows should not only be about your view but should be strategically placed to help minimize heat/cold loss and, if desired, passive solar gain. Every window and door buck should have a strong, thick lintel above it spanning no shorter than 12" past on both sides above. There should be at least a 1/4" gap between the buck and the lintel to allow for future settling.

Make sure when placing your door bucks that you place them high enough for the bottom jam to come out at a comfortable height to join with your final flooring.

This is an example of an exceptionally large door buck that will hold two windows either side of a large door.

You can get highly creative with your doors and windows. I have seen all kinds of shapes and beautiful designs. That being said, there are a few things to remember to help your windows be an asset and not an ongoing do over.

The biggest mess comes from using metal framed windows. Metal window frames are notorious for sweating and condensation. This in turn creates damp walls and an extremely considerable risk of mold issues, especially with straw bales. Try to stay with wood or vinyl frames. I have seen a lot of people use sheets of glass (unframed) and cob them right into the wall. This gives a wonderful opportunity for creating whatever shape window you want. Unfortunately, most of the time the force and shrinkage of the drying cob, or shifting weight causes the glass to shatter or crack. To prevent this, you can create a buck to go around it. The buck can be a square around a circle of glass.

The purpose of the buck is just to take most of the weight and movement instead of it being totally on the glass. Remember you will still put a lintel over your buck! So far, we have not had a single unframed glass break on us using this method.

This is a good example of a window buck made specifically to be installed in straw bales. Note the porcupine wings extending from the bottom.

When designing your front door (main entrance) you want to make it the star of your build. When someone looks at your home, it should tell them, "Here is my entrance!" Your entrance should be grand and inviting. There should be no doubt of where to go, unless of course you are trying to deter visitors from approaching, and that can be done too! Your door does not have to be store bought, it can be hand-crafted by you or a friend. Your door can be arched, round, Dutch, or traditional. Have fun with it! After all, it is the first thing you see walking up to your house. Just remember to take your time and think about placement carefully before you commit to it.

Common Mistakes with Door and Window

- Placing doors and windows before figuring datum (final floor height)
- Using metal window frames
- Improper or lack of bracing on window and door bucks, resulting in twisted out of level/plumb windows
- Forgetting to install lintels above windows and doors
- Not spanning lintels at least 12" beyond both sides of the top of the buck

Notes and Sketches

Tools and Hacks

Don't forget that nothing good comes easy. It is always helpful to have the right tools for the job. Take mixing cob as an example:
Mixing your cob by foot on a tarp can be very grounding, but it is also very time consuming.

Miguelito and Adriana are pictured mixing cob on tarp with bare feet.

I couldn't have done a build this big without my backhoe, Big Stinky!

There are many tools that will help you with your build:

- Buckets (5 gallon)
- Chain saw
- Cob Saws
- Cobbing gloves
- Cobber's thumb
- Daisy
- Hard Rake
- Levels (2ft and 4ft - 6ft)
- Masons Brush (large)
- Pocket Knife
- Scaffolding
- Shovels
- Tape Measure
- Torpedo Level
- Wheelbarrow (heavy duty) (preferred 2 wheels)

Making a Cob Saw for Trimming

This cob saw was created by using a grinder to enlarge the teeth on an old hand saw. This is ideal for plumbing the sides of your walls.

Making a "Daisy"

The daisy is made using an old circular saw blade that has the teeth grinded off it with a grinder. A metal pipe is then welded to the center creating a handle as seen above. This tool is a must have for hacking away dried cob from a wall. Cob is extremely hard when it is dry, and this tool not only makes the removal a lot easier, but also the amount taken off can be controlled by how you aim the blade. This is one of my favorite natural building hack tools.

Making a "Cobber's Thumb"

This is the least expensive of all of your tools, grab a 1" thick branch or stick and slightly round off one end. This can be done even by scraping it on a firm surface. Also, if you have access to deer antlers, they work great for cobblers' thumbs. This tool is used a lot in wet humid areas to create air holes in the cob wall to help it dry faster. The holes also give your plaster something to adhere to.

Making a Tapered Level

Using a 4ft level and assuming you are tapering a 1/2" per foot, you will need to duct tape a piece of wood to your level that has one end 2" wider than the other from one of the levels to the other. This is creating a 1/2" per foot difference at a 4ft span.

Making Scaffolding

This scaffolding can be made from scrap wood or even live edge lumber. These can be made at any height giving you a sturdy advantage to cob a lot higher without a ladder. Depending on what you use running across the top it is strong enough to hold a backhoe load of cob along with your weight.

Notes and Sketches

Testimonials

I arrived at Cob Hill in complete awe of the daunting scale of the building project and the speed with which it was actually being accomplished. It was clear beyond doubt that Cat was a power horse. Young people, circling around her, eager to learn and help, watched as she mounted her backhoe to mix yet another enormous batch of cob from the hillside's clay-rich soil or as she wielded her chainsaw to fell a giant timber from the surrounding woods. Filled with determination and earthly practicality, Cat was there to show the world how to build dreams from the depths of pure passion and undying love. I left Cob Hill with renewed inspiration and gratitude that people like Cat existed.

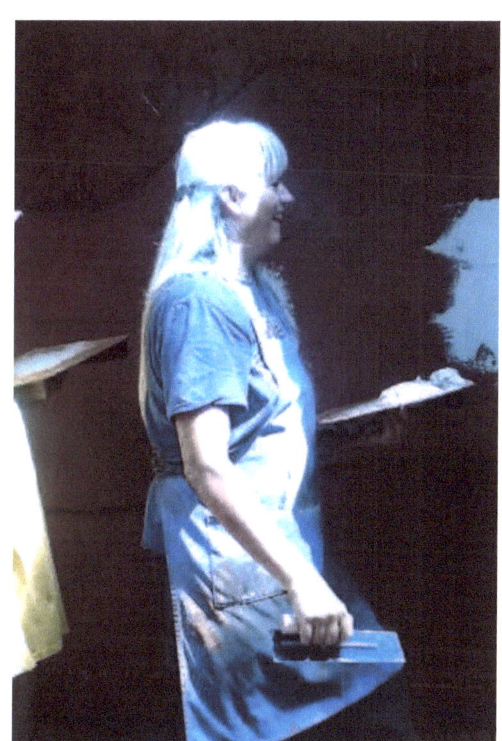

Athena Steen, CaneloProject.com

It's a joy to work with Cat. Her lighthearted smile and playful antics make even the hardest of tasks into a heartwarming experience. Cat has been a natural building mentor of mine for three years now. She immediately welcomed me into this community of builders and has connected me to many other amazing people through her workshops. Anyone that has had the privilege to meet Cat at Cob Hill can see what a caring and nurturing person Cat is. Cob Hill is a beautiful, ever-evolving, safe space for people from all walks of life to reconnect to nature on many levels and it's all because of the unstoppable woman that is Cat Taylor.

Jess Shockley,
Terrabellum.org and
TexasHealthyHomes.com

Cheryl Gorn, Homeowner

I can't stress enough what a fantastic teacher Cat Taylor is. I met her on a build in Oregon, where I was utterly confused about this natural building thing. She told me repeatedly, natural building isn't rocket science, and that the way to learn it is by doing. Cat shared with me how to do some particular techniques and then had me do them myself, helping me along until I caught on. Cat is not only a terrific teacher, she is also a fun, gracious person with a huge heart.

I hired Cat Taylor to come and help
me with my build spring of 2021. I
had hoped to attend a workshop in
2020/2021 but any workshop I had
been interested in had been canceled
due to COVID. Cat was more than
willing to drive from Texas to Idaho to
spend 10 days teaching and guiding
us with her wealth of experience and
knowledge. I was SO grateful to have
her come to my build site, to give her
personal instruction was exactly what
I needed at the time, and when she
left, she left me/us with a wealth of
information to keep us going even
after she was gone. Not only did Cat
contribute to my understanding of
how to build a bale/cob home, she
worked tirelessly beside us every day
for 10-hour days in order to complete
as much as possible before she
returned to Texas. She became a
friend and mud sister over those 10
days as well with her open heart,
endless smile and willingness to
share not only her knowing of natural
building, but giving of her Self. I will
forever be grateful for that time and
her continued support and friendship.

Kaye La Bella, Homeowner

Glossary of Terms

(AKA: Vo-cob-ulary)

Adobe: Earthen brick, clay sand and straw put into a brick shaped form and dried in the sun. Adobe is the same thing as cob, except in brick form.

Bale/Cob: A hybrid form of natural building using straw bales brick stacked and stacked into the center of a cob wall. The straw acts as an insulator for the cob wall structure. This is prime for areas of extreme heat or cold.

Buttress: A solid strong structure designed to support a wall.

Cement: Although it is not considered a "natural" product, I have included it for those who are not aware. Cement is a binder and is used in construction. The manufacturing of cement produces about 0.9 pounds of CO_2 for every pound of cement which in turn creates 8% of the world's CO_2 emission.

Clay slip: A mix of water and clay creating a gravy thickness for applying on any non-cob parts of your build you need to apply cob. Also used for light straw clay.

Cob: A mixture of clay soil, sand, straw and water. The meaning of the word cob is Welsh for lump.

Cobalanche: A term given to the collapse of a cob wall. Usually resulting from going up to too fast and not allowing dry time, or failure to trim and plumb walls. These can be extremely dangerous; cob easily weighs thousands of pounds.

Cobalicious: A cob structure that looks so good you could just eat it up!

Cobateria: The name given to the community kitchen/cafeteria at Cob Hill Natural Building School.

Cobber's Thumb: A ¾" to 1" thick stick rounded at the end, used to poke out holes in a cob wall to expedite drying time in wet humid areas.

Cob Gobbler: A person that applies cob to the wall faster than a person can throw it to them. Also, a description of the mysterious monster that lives by the big pond at Cob Hill. This monster is responsible for keeping the small children from venturing to the water by themselves.

Cobin: A small Cob cottage that is designed for one or two people for short stays.

Cob Line: A line of people starting at a cob source and ending at a cob wall being built. The idea is to "toss" the cob down the line of people to the person on the wall.

Cob Pit: The hole created when using a **backhoe** to dig for clay creating a perfect "bowl" for mixing cob.

Cob Saw: Made from old antique hand saws, the cobber's saw has the teeth ground off to create large triangles to trim the excess cob off the sides of the wall while building. This in turn keeps the walls "plumb".

Cordwood: A section of tree cut into short pieces of log. The logs are cut to the length of the desired thickness of a wall. Cordwood must be seasoned and allowed to fully dry before using in a wall system or it may create gaps later. Cordwood walls can be mortared with cob, hempcrete or mortar.

Cupola: An "upside down" cup like hollow framed structure that sits on steep roofs or entered over the holed center of a reciprocal roof system, sometimes referred to as a steeple.

Daisy: A tool used to hack off large amounts of protruding dried cob. This tool cuts through the hardened cob. This tool cuts through the hardened cob, a saw cannot. Usually made from a grinded down 7¼" circular saw blade welded to a 12" piece of metal pipe.

Datum: The starting point for measuring your ceiling height. Also nicknamed your final floor height.

Deadman: Unlike it sounds, a deadman is a piece of wood placed into a cob wall for attaching things to, such as cabinets, hanging TVs, or heavy mirrors. Also used to tie in roofing to the walls in heavy wind areas.

Dimensional: In natural building this refers to store bought or squared up pieces of lumber, such as 2 x 6, versus round logs.

Door buck: A large wide heavy-duty frame made to be inserted into a cob or natural built wall to attach a door into when the wall is completed.

Drain rock: Course rock used to allow water to run/drain through. Usually around 2" in diameter but can come smaller and be up to 3½" bigger.

Draw Knife: A heavy blade with a handle on each end. This is used to peel bark off trees after they have been harvested. The knife is dragged along the bark by "drawing" it toward you using both hands resulting in bark removal.

Dry Stacking: The art of creating a stone wall without the use of mortar or cement. Each rock is carefully placed to support the next, locking them together.

Flex Base: Primarily used for road base, it is a mix of gravel, clay and limestone. Flex base tamps down and keeps its form indefinitely. Rain or water helps it to harden permanently in place. It is commonly used as the final top foundation layer in natural builds.

Heartening: Also called "fines". These are granite chips of rock, usually 1" or less in size. This is used to help lock rocks on dry stacked stem walls.

Joist: A joist is the log or dimensional lumber (or metal) that spans horizontally across the span of your ceiling/roof reaching and connecting to the outer walls.

Level: A description of something being the same height at either horizontal end. It is also what the tool is called that is used to find or adjust a level surface.

Light straw clay(lsc): This is a process of using a temporary form to infill a wall system. Straw is placed on a tarp, adding small amounts of clay slip. The straw is then "tossed" like a salad until all the straw is lightly coated in slip. A piece of plywood is temporarily screwed to the interior of the wall and straw is packed into the space. The board is removed and moved up repeating the process to the top of the wall.

Lime Pointing: The application of lime mortar (sand, lime, water) to fill between existing structures seems, such as between the outside crevices of a dry stacked stem wall. This is often done with a "pointed" trowel to help fill smaller spaces efficiently.

Lintel: A lintel is a large thick strong span of wood or metal used above openings such as windows, doors and archways, allowing the weight from above to be dispersed to the outside edges of opening, taking the weight off window or door opening.

Live edge: A piece of wood that has been sliced off a log by a mill, but the edges have not been straightened with a saw. This results in a flat piece with the edges still being the original shape of the tree.

Palletable Cob: This is a style of natural building made popular by Miguel Elliott, using wooden pallets as wall structures, that are then stuffed with straw and covered with cob.

Passive Solar: A building design that collects solar heat from the sun when needed and reflects away heat when not wanted.

Perforated drainpipe: Usually, but not always, a flexible accordion style plastic pipe with holes perforated through it. This pipe can be 4" to 6" wide. It is even available in a wider width in some areas. The perforation allows water to enter the pipe easily to run out the lower end.

Permeable: Means a material that allows gas or liquids to pass through it.

Plaster: The decorative and protective layer applied as a final coat on walls and other structures needing a final coat. This can also use to make 3-dimensional art on walls.

Plumb: A description of something running straight up and down in a vertical position.

Porcupine: A piece of wood, usually a short log, with nails hammered into it protruding out causing it to look like a porcupine. These are used to place into the top, middle and bottom of door and window openings to give a stable spot to attach window and door bucks. The nails embed in the cob locking it in forever.

Rubble Trench: Part of the foundation base of a stem wall, the rubble trench is a trench usually as deep as the frost line and varying in width from 18" to up to 3ft, depending on the size of the walls. The trench is lined with landscape fabric to filter out silt and earth. The trench has 4" to 6" perforated drainpipe at the bottom to increase excess flow of water away from the walls. The trench is then filled with tamped drain rock, landscape fabric folded over the top, and stem wall built on top

Sheathing: The first covering on the outside of your walls or on your roof, usually on your roofing joists, this can be plywood, live edge or dimensional.

Septic: This is a black water system designed to safely dispose and break down urine and feces coming from toilets. The septic system usually has two 500-gallon concrete tanks and a large leach field of stone and perforated drainpipe.

Stem wall: The bottom base of a wall system, separating the wall material from the ground supplying a strong support and protecting it from the elements of ground exposure. The stem wall is commonly made from materials such as rock, urbanite, or concrete.

Straw Bale: Unlike "hay" straw is not a food or even organic. Straw is the empty shell of the stalk of a dead wheat plant. After cutting the wheat head off the top the stalk is then chopped off and bailed. It is made of silica and the hollow stalk makes a great insulation material. The straw is also used for tensile strength in cob mix, like rebar in concrete

Tamper: A tamper is a tool used to pack down earth or gravel firmly. The tool has a square 8" to 10" flat piece of wooden handle. There is also a hydraulic tamping machine that you walk behind and push. This is good for larger areas that would be too much for tamping by hand.

Thermal Mass: The ability for a material to absorb, store and release heat. Cob is a good example of a thermal mass material.

Trombe Wall: A wall made of thermal mass material placed inside a window where it can absorb heat from the sun. Usually made of cob and built as a partial/pony wall.

Urbanite: A nickname given to broken pieces of used concrete. This is often used for stem wall construction because of the low cost and reuse/recycle ability.

Vapor Barrier: A material that is completely waterproof, such as heavy plastic, asphalt paper, pond liner and some heavy-duty tarps.

Wattle and Daub: One of the oldest methods of natural building. The process of weaving thin branches, bamboo or pieces of wood creating a wall structure to then fill in with cob.

Window Buck: A thick heavy wood frame placed into the wall for the installation of a window later in the build process.

About the Author

Cob Hill was founded in 2018 by Cat Taylor after working in modern construction and remodeling for over 25 years. Although building was one of her main sources of income, her hobby and true talent has always been as an artist and sculptor.

In 2015 Cat was designing a natural swimming pool when she discovered cob. It was then that natural building became her main focus. Unfortunately, a breast cancer diagnosis delayed her hands-on experience for two years. As soon as she was strong enough, she attended her first cob workshop and immediately broke ground on the cob house that started it all. She facilitated her first workshop in 2018. A widow of a veteran who suffered from PTSD, Cat combined her already existing natural building school with NaturalBuildingOrg, a 501(c3) non-profit organization. This non-profit began a slate of educational and therapeutic programs to empower all who wish to heal, grow and live in harmony with the earth. Serving Veterans by giving them the education, guidance, and assistance in building their own mortgage free home at little or no cost.

Website: https://www.cobhillnaturalbuilding.com/

Facebook: https://www.facebook.com/cobhillnaturalbuildingschool

Email: cobhill.naturalbuildingschool@gmail.com

Cob Hill Natural Building School
Hughes Springs
Texas, 75656